WORLD FOOD

Hungary

Find our books at Amazon, Barnes & Nobles, Walmart,
Books-A-Million, OverDrive, Kobo, Lulu and more!

Like, Share and Follow us on Facebook, Instagram, Threads,
Pinterest, YouTube, LinkedIn, and more! Find our Sloths Love to
Read Podcast on Spotify, Apple Podcast. Amazon Music, and more!

www.SlothDreamsBooks.com

Hungary

WRITTEN BY ROY JELINEK
ILLUSTRATED BY KERIANNE JELINEK

Gulyás

GOULASH SOUP

Paprikás Csirke

CHICKEN PAPRIKA

Töltött Paprika

STUFFED PEPPERS

Lángos

FRIED BREAD

Palacsinta

CREPES

Dobos Torta

DRUM CAKE

Pörkölt

BEEF STEW

Rakott Krumpli

POTATO CASSEROLE

Töltött Káposzta
STUFFED CABBAGE

Téli Salami
WINTER SALAMI

Kolbász

SAUSAGE

Véres Hurka

BLOOD SAUSAGE

Meggyleves
CHERRY SOUP

Lecsó

STEW

Túrós Csusza

CREAMY NOODLES

Húsleves

BEEF SOUP

Nokedli

DUMPLINGS

Kürtőskalács

CHIMNEY CAKE

Beigli

CHRISTMAS CAKE

Főzelék

THICK STEW

Halászlé

FISHERMAN'S SOUP

Rétes

STRUDEL

Eszterházy Torta

ESZTERHAZY CAKE

Szilvas Gomboc

PLUM DUMPLINGS

Zserbó
GERBEAUD CAKE

Almas Pite

APPLE CAKE